Laurie Rozakis, Ph.D.

Troll Associates

Interior Illustrations by: Elliot Kreloff

ISBN: 0-8167-2589-6

Printed in the United States of America.

10 9 8 7 6 5 4 3 2

Contents

GRADES 4–6

Introduction

Read it! Write it! Ideas to Integrate Writing and Literature offers you a wealth of teacher-tested ways to reinforce writing skills and nurture a love of fine literature in your students. A complete overview of each book, lively student-centered class activities, and creative activity sheets provide you with a complete guide to expanding your students' literary horizons.

Read it! Write it! Ideas to Integrate Writing and Literature is divided into two sections by level. The first section is designed for use with students in kindergarten through grade three. There are 23 books represented in this section, arranged alphabetically by title for ease of use. Many forms of literature are represented, including wordless books, picture books, folk and fairy tales, rhyme, and repetition stories. Among the titles included are such traditional favorites as *The Carrot Seed, Frog and Toad Together, Goodnight Moon, The Gingerbread Boy,* and *Shake My Sillies Out* as well as such recent award-winning works as *Lon Po Po* and *Hershel and the Hanukkah Goblins.* The second section contains 22 books for use with students in grades four through six. As with the first section, the books are arranged alphabetically by title. The titles represent a wide variety of genres such as novels, poetry, nonfiction, and historical fiction. The titles include *Dear Mr. Henshaw, Island of the Blue Dolphins, Jacob Have I Loved, Tales Mummies Tell, Number the Stars,* and *Wilma Rudolph: Champion Athlete.*

Represented are some of the most popular authors in children's literature: Beverly Cleary, Jean Craighead George, Gail Gibbons, Virginia Hamilton, Patricia Lauber, Arnold Lobel, Lois Lowry, Scott O'Dell, Katherine Paterson, Cynthia Rylant, Mildred D. Taylor, Chris Van Allsburg, Cynthia Voigt, E. B. White, and Ed Young. The selection of literature is multicultural by virtue of characters and authors.

Each book is accorded two pages; the first page contains a complete citation, including author, publisher, and place and date of publication, followed by a concise summary of the plot, a listing of awards and prizes the book has won, and a class activity. The remaining page contains a class activity specifically tailored to the work under study. These activities provide you with many different ways to integrate writing and literature and help foster your students' love of reading. Among the activities are poetry, song-writing, puppetry, diaries, letters, new story endings, birthday and thank-you cards, student-made books, game making, and critical reviews. These different activities also give you a way to integrate material from other content areas. For example, an activity on Verna Aardema's *Bringing the Rain to Kapiti Plain: A Nandi Tale* challenges students to sharpen their geography and science skills through a study of weather patterns; an activity on Ruth Krauss's *The Carrot Seed* reinforces math skills through charting and graphing.

Most of all these activities are designed to be fun! From creating a class story, staging a story reading, and holding read-aloud events in the school and community to creating improvisations and designing advertising campaigns, students will be intrigued by the possibilities inherent in reading and responding to literature.

Read it! Write it! Ideas to Integrate Writing and Literature offers you imaginative and exciting ways to guide your students' love of reading and writing. Enjoy!

The Bremen Town Musicians

JACOB AND WILHELM GRIMM
RETOLD BY DAVID CUTTS
(TROLL ASSOCIATES, 1979)

ALL ABOUT THE BOOK

In *The Bremen Town Musicians,* various animals travel to the town of Bremen, hoping to be musicians there. On their way they come to a house and in it they see robbers sitting around a table enjoying a great feast. The hungry musicians trick the robbers into leaving the house and enjoy the feast themselves. The musicians happily settle in the house.

CLASS ACTIVITY

Have students write a song for the "[Name of your town] Musicians" to perform. Begin with a familiar tune, such as "Row, Row, Row Your Boat" or "Frère Jacques." Then have students substitute their own words to create a song that expresses something about them and their class. Encourage students to use familiar rhymes, such as *June/moon/tune/noon,* to help them remember the song. Then have students make simple instruments, such as drums from coffee cans, to accompany their song. Perform the song while marching around the classroom.

NAME ______________________________ DATE ____________

Music Lessons

Below are pictures of musical instruments and their names. Unscramble the name of each instrument. Then write the name of each instrument under its picture. In each bubble, write a word that tells about the sound each instrument makes.

elutf	mruds	tearinlc
niloiv	buat	oianp

Bringing the Rain to Kapiti Plain: A Nandi Tale

VERNA AARDEMA
(NEW YORK: THE DIAL PRESS, 1981)

ALL ABOUT THE BOOK

Ki-pat sees the drought around him in *Bringing the Rain to Kapiti Plain: A Nandi Tale.* Using an eagle's feather for an arrow, he aims at the cloudy sky. The feather pierces the cloud and causes the rain to fall.

CLASS ACTIVITY

On one level, *Bringing the Rain to Kapiti Plain* concerns the potentially life-threatening effects of drought. Discuss with students how different areas of the country have different weather patterns. It could be snowing in Vermont, for example, while people in southern Florida are swimming in their outdoor pools. Extend the discussion to include the world as well. Using a large world map, have students identify different weather patterns in different parts of the world. Begin with well-known places such as the North and South Poles, and add other regions depending on your students' grade and ability levels. You might want to mention areas that suffer from hurricanes, such as the Caribbean Islands, and places that have tornadoes, such as Kansas.

NAME ______________________________ DATE ______________

Rain, Rain, Come This Day!

Ki-pat made rain by shooting an eagle's feather at a cloud. If you were Ki-pat, how would you make rain fall? Would you say special words? Would you sing a song? Would you use anything special?

On the lines below, write a sentence that tells how you would make the rain come. Then draw a picture that shows what you would do.

____

____

Brother to the Wind

MILDRED PITTS WALTER
(NEW YORK: LOTHROP, LEE & SHEPARD BOOKS, 1985)

ALL ABOUT THE BOOK

Brother to the Wind describes Emeke's travels from his village of Eronni to find Good Snake. He asks Good Snake to grant him his wish to fly. Good Snake tells him to get the bark of a baobab tree and three large bamboo poles. Emeke then makes a kite exactly like the one on the back of a rock Good Snake gives him. Although Emeke's parents and elders laugh at him, he takes the kite to the edge of the mountain where it enables him to soar.

CLASS ACTIVITY

The book revolves around Emeke's efforts to make a special kite. Have students make kites of their own. Start with dowels, sheets of plain white or brown paper, string, and fabric scraps. For each kite, cross two dowels and secure them with glue. Hot glue guns, available for a nominal price at a hardware, craft, or sewing store, work especially well. Then have each student secure the paper on his or her kite, using staples. Encourage students to decorate their kites with crayons and markers, making the kites as special as Emeke's. Make a tail by tying fabric strips onto string. Then punch a hole through the paper at one end of the kite and tie the tail through it. Attach a long string to dowel for flying the kite. Fly the kites as a class on a bright and clear day when it is moderately windy.

NAME ____________________ DATE __________

My Picture Book

Read the sentence in each box. Draw a picture about it. Then cut out the boxes. Put them in the correct order. Staple the pages together. You will have your own picture book about Emeke and Good Snake!

Emeke flies his kite.	Good Snake gives Emeke a rock.
Emeke gets the bark of a baobab tree and three large bamboo poles.	Emeke goes to find Good Snake.
Emeke makes a kite.	Emeke finds Good Snake.

The Carrot Seed

RUTH KRAUSS
(NEW YORK: HARPER & ROW, 1945)

ALL ABOUT THE BOOK

A little boy plants a seed and waits for it to grow in *The Carrot Seed.* His family is interested, but not encouraging. Still, the boy cares for the plant and finally is rewarded with a carrot so large that he must move it in a wheelbarrow.

CLASS ACTIVITY

Much of the appeal of this book derives from the element of surprise: the smallest person grows the biggest carrot. To help students appreciate size differences, have them measure commonplace items in their class. To take their measurements, students can use any measuring tool they wish, such as a conventional ruler, or even their thumb or handspan, for example. Then create a class measurement chart to record their findings. Encourage students to use metric measurements as well as English measurements on their chart.

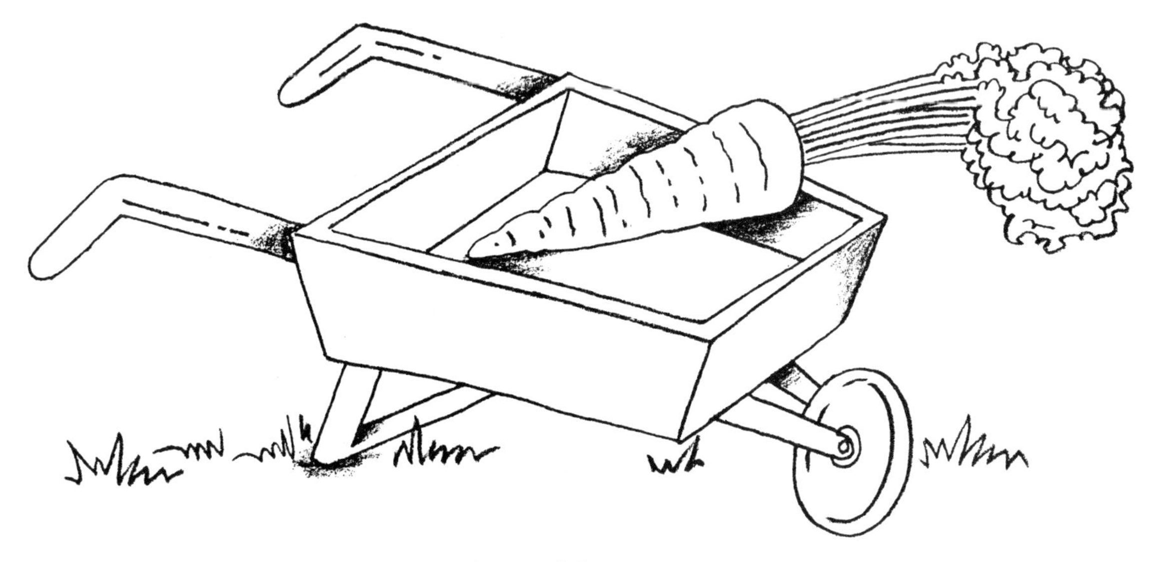

NAME ______________________________ DATE ____________

What a Carrot!

Below are five steps a boy followed to grow a carrot. Put the steps in order. Write 1 in the box under the first step, 2 in the box under the second step, and so on. Then color the pictures.

He carried the carrot away.

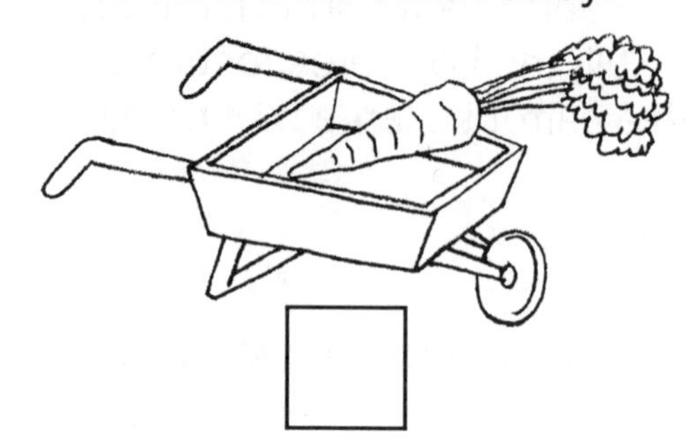

He picked the carrot.

He raked the ground.

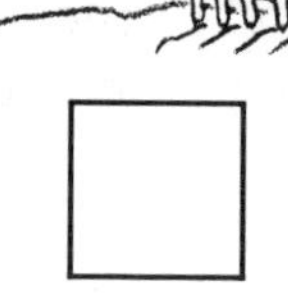

He watered the seed.

He planted a seed.

Cinderella

TRANSLATED BY CHARLES PERRAULT
PICTURES BY MARCIA BROWN
(NEW YORK: CHARLES SCRIBNER'S SONS, 1954)

ALL ABOUT THE BOOK

This beautifully illustrated version of *Cinderella*, the classic tale of the mistreated maiden who triumphs through her goodness (and the help of her fairy godmother!), won the 1955 Caldecott Medal.

CLASS ACTIVITY

Recast *Cinderella* into a puppet play. First, have students work together to create puppets representing all the main characters. They can create puppets from simple line drawing cutouts mounted on craft sticks or fabric scraps glued to socks, for example. As a class, prepare the puppet stage. A table draped with fabric or paper works well. Then assign students various speaking parts, rotating the cast so that everyone has a chance to play a role. Students can read directly from the book, or they can retell the story in their own words. Perform the puppet show for parents, a class of younger students, or senior citizens. Ask the school's media specialist or a parent volunteer to videotape the production so that students can watch it later.

NAME ______________________ DATE ____________

And They Lived Happily Ever After?

Cinderella and the prince live happily ever after—or do they? Tell what happens to Cinderella and the prince after they marry. Do they have children? Move to another place? Write your thoughts on these lines.

Fossils Tell of Long Ago

ALIKI
(NEW YORK: HARPER, 1990)

ALL ABOUT THE BOOK

Fossils Tell of Long Ago opens with the explanation that a fossil is anything that has been preserved that can tell us about life on earth millions of years ago. The author then discusses how fossils tell us about the strange and fascinating plant and animal life that once covered the earth. She also provides instructions for readers to make their own "fossils."

CLASS ACTIVITY

Aliki explains how to make a clay print of our hands so people hundreds of years in the future will know something about us. Extend this activity by inviting students to make clay "fossils" of objects considered important in today's culture. Begin by discussing with students which objects from our lives might tell people in the future something about the way we live. Then ask each student to bring in three different objects worthy of preservation. These can be such things as little robot toys, soda bottles, or fast-food containers. As a class, select one object for each student to use as a "fossil." Make a clear clay imprint of the object. Then have each student write a brief paragraph explaining what this object might tell future people about the way we live.

NAME ______________________ DATE __________

New Discoveries!

Imagine that you found the fossils pictured below. What do they tell you about things that lived in the past? For each fossil, write two things it might tell you. Here's an example to get you started:

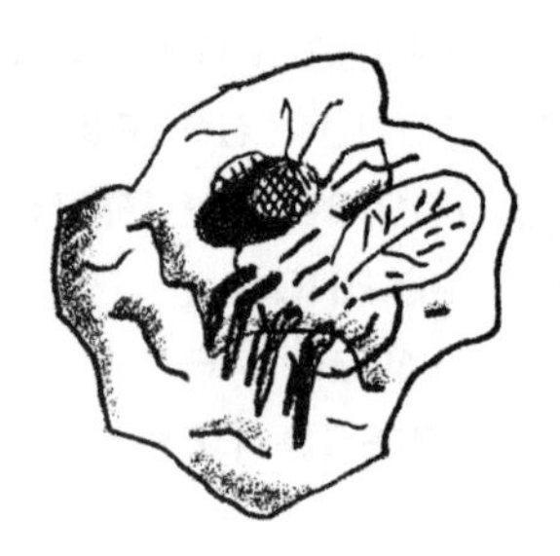

1. This insect lived on or near the trees.
2. The insect probably got trapped in the tree sap because it moved slowly.

1. ____________________
2. ____________________

1. ____________________
2. ____________________

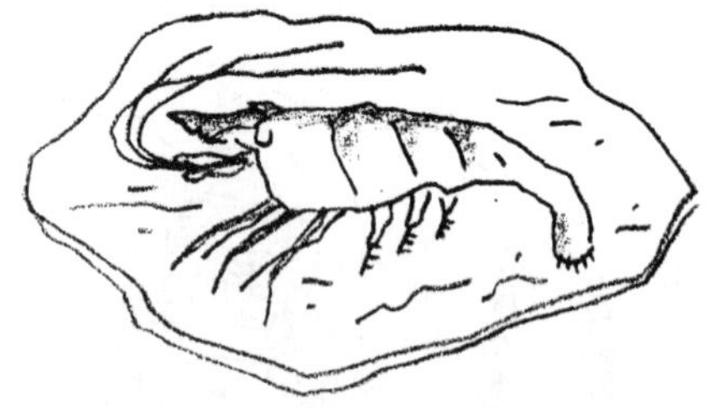

1. ____________________
2. ____________________

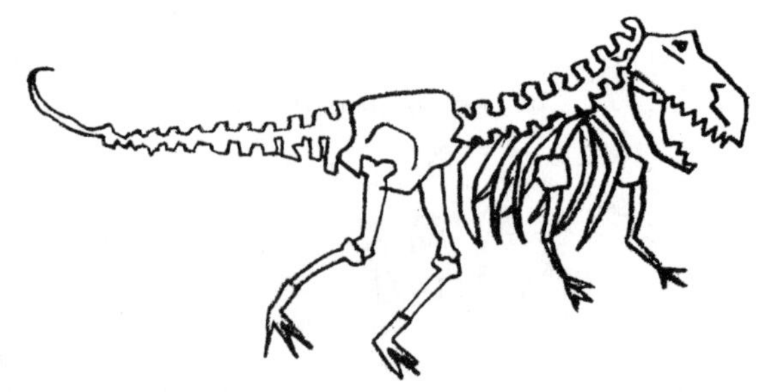

1. ____________________
2. ____________________

Frog and Toad Together

ARNOLD LOBEL
(NEW YORK: HARPER & ROW, 1979)

ALL ABOUT THE BOOK

This 1973 Newbery Honor Book, *Frog and Toad Together,* contains five stories about the good friends, Frog and Toad. "A List" tells all the things Toad plans to do in a day—a good idea until he loses his list. In "The Garden," Frog advises Toad how to grow a garden as splendid as his own. The friends test their will power in "Cookies" and find the depths of their bravery in "Dragons and Giants." "The Dream" makes a star of Toad, and teaches him to appreciate Frog.

CLASS ACTIVITY

As a class, challenge students to write another adventure story for Frog and Toad. Begin by asking children to brainstorm ideas for the story. Encourage them to keep to the characterizations that Lobel created for Frog and Toad. The plot should concern an everyday incident rather than an unusual or extraordinary event. When the entire class has helped develop the plot, ask children to suggest lines, one at a time. Use a bright crayon or magic marker to write students' suggestions on a large piece of butcher paper. When the story is complete, read it back to the children. Then encourage groups of students to illustrate the story. Share the completed story with the class and with others.

NAME ________________________ DATE ____________

Happy Birthday to You!

Happy birthday to Frog! Happy birthday to Toad! Make a birthday card for Frog or for Toad. Draw a birthday picture. Write a special birthday wish for Frog or Toad. Don't forget to sign your name!

The Funny Little Woman

ARLENE MOSEL
ILLUSTRATED BY BLAIR LENT
(NEW YORK: E.P. DUTTON, 1972)

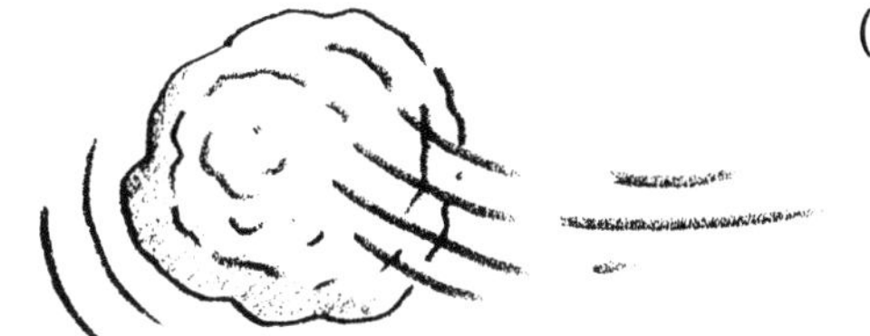

ALL ABOUT THE BOOK

In *The Funny Little Woman,* a woman makes a rice dumpling that rolls away from her. When she chases it, she ends up a prisoner of the oni, wicked creatures that live underground. For his illustrations, Blair Lent received the 1973 Caldecott Medal.

CLASS ACTIVITY

Have students follow a simple recipe to create dumplings. The recipe on a commercial biscuit mix works well with younger children. Copy the recipe from the side of the box onto the chalkboard. Have students read the recipe as they mix the biscuit mix and water. As you cook the dumplings in boiling water, have students clean up. Enjoy!

NAME ____________________ DATE ____________

Soup's On

The funny little woman makes a rice dumpling. What foods do you like to make? A peanut-butter-and-jelly sandwich? Scrambled eggs? Write a recipe for making your favorite food. First list the ingredients you need. Then list the steps you have to follow to make this dish.

The food I am going to make is called ____________________.

I need the following ingredients:

____________________ ____________________

____________________ ____________________

____________________ ____________________

Here are the steps:

1. ____________________

2. ____________________

3. ____________________

4. ____________________

The Gingerbread Boy

JAKOB GRIMM AND WILHELM K. GRIMM
RETOLD BY DAVID CUTTS
(TROLL ASSOCIATES, 1979)

ALL ABOUT THE BOOK

The Gingerbread Boy tells about a little old woman who bakes a gingerbread boy. The boy jumps out of the oven and runs away. The woman and her husband chase the gingerbread boy. As they run, the animals and people they pass join in the chase. The gingerbread boy comes to a fox, who tricks him and eats him.

CLASS ACTIVITY

A few days before the activity, arrange for students to tour the school building, ending at the library. The day of the activity, have each student make a gingerbread boy or girl from brown construction paper, adding facial features with crayons or markers. When the class leaves the classroom for lunch, take all the gingerbread figures to the library. As students return from lunch and notice their figures missing, explore where the gingerbread people might have gone. Look for them by touring the school. This is a good chance to introduce students to such people as the principal, the nurse, the secretaries, and the teachers' aides. Complete your "search" at the library, where you have left the gingerbread people. You might want to read the book aloud to students again, as well as other tales by the Grimm brothers.

NAME ______________________________ DATE ______________

Around the World

The gingerbread boy tries to outrace everyone in the town. How far do you think he would have gone if the fox had not caught him? Do you think he could have gone around the world?

Imagine that *you* could go around the world. First use your finger to trace different routes on the world map below. When you have chosen the way you want to go, draw your path. Then draw five different ways you could travel, such as by car or balloon!

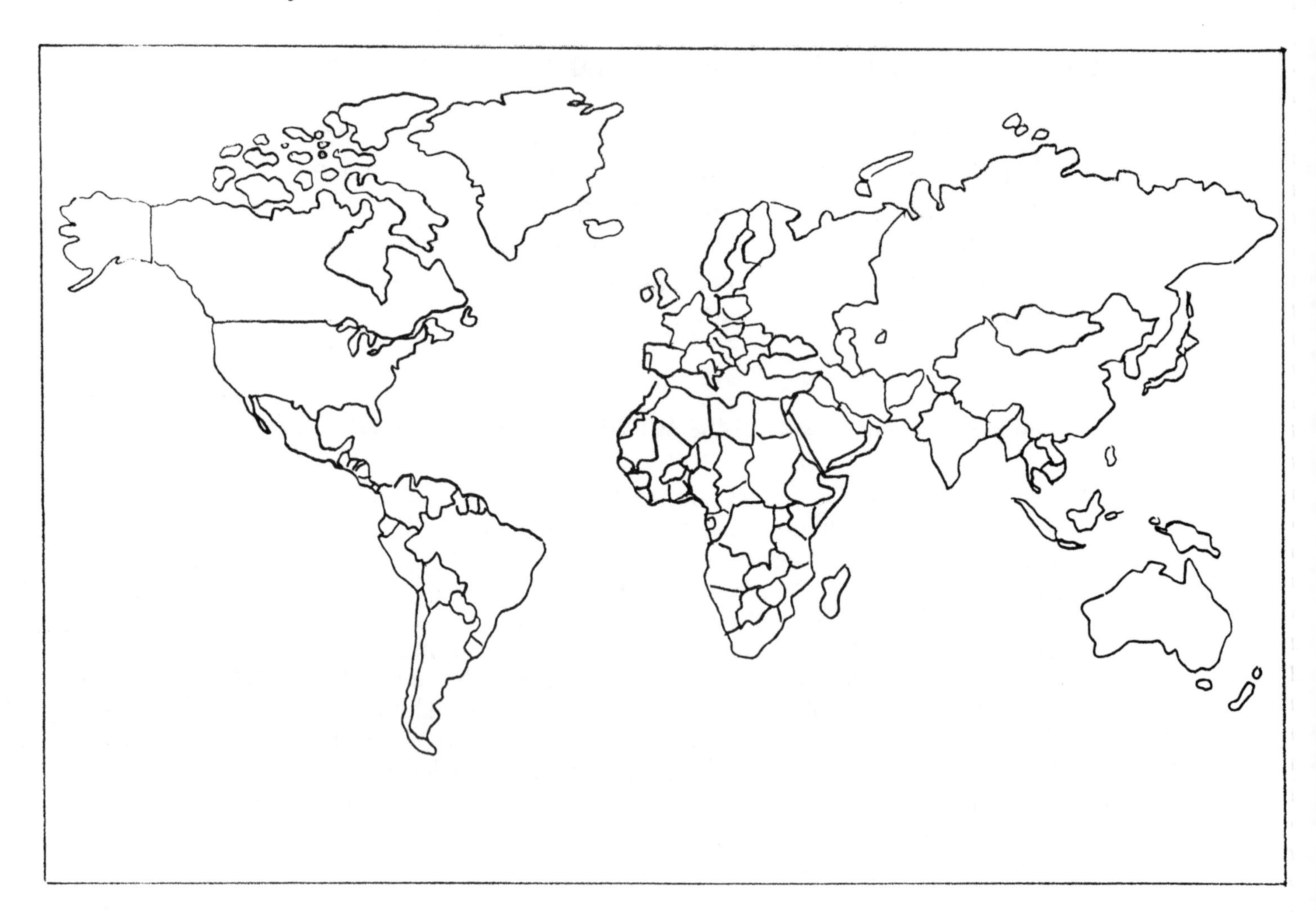

Goodnight Moon

MARGARET WISE BROWN
(NEW YORK: HARPER & ROW, 1947)

ALL ABOUT THE BOOK

In this classic bedtime book, *Goodnight Moon,* a little rabbit looks around the room and says "goodnight" to familiar items, such as his toys and furniture.

CLASS ACTIVITY

Goodnight Moon derives much of its appeal from the sounds of the words as well as the charm of the everyday objects. Have students write a poem similar to a cinquain as a way of exploring the effects of words and their sounds. Begin by writing the form of the cinquain and a sample on the board:

Form	*Sample*
Line 1: one word (may be the title)	Bear
Line 2: two words (describing the title)	Soft, brown
Line 3: three words (an action)	Cuddles at night
Line 4: four words (a feeling)	I like to hold
Line 5: one word (referring to the title)	Nice

Then have students select an object in their bedroom that they especially like—a stuffed toy, a night light, a book, a blanket, and so forth. Guide students to express their feelings about the object in the cinquain form. To help students hear the sounds of the words they are using, encourage them to say the words aloud softly as they write. When everyone is finished, have students share their poems with the class.

NAME ______________________________ DATE ______________

My Goodnight Book

Make your own book of things you see before going to sleep. Write a word to complete each sentence. Draw a picture of the word you wrote. Then cut the sentences apart. Staple the pages. You will have your own goodnight book!

1. Goodnight ______________________.

4. Goodnight ______________________.

2. Goodnight ______________________.

5. Goodnight ______________________.

3. Goodnight ______________________.

6. Goodnight ______________________.

Gorilla

ANTHONY BROWNE
(NEW YORK: ALFRED A. KNOPF, 1983)

ALL ABOUT THE BOOK

Hannah loves gorillas. She asks her father to take her to the zoo to see them, but he does not have the time. She asks her father for a gorilla for her birthday. The night before her birthday, she awakens to find a stuffed gorilla at the foot of her bed. She throws the gorilla in the corner and goes back to sleep. She dreams the gorilla comes alive and takes her to the zoo, to the movies, and to a place to eat. The next morning Hannah awakens to find the toy gorilla on her pillow. For her birthday, Hannah's father takes her to the zoo to see the gorilla. *Gorilla* won the 1984 Kate Greenaway Medal.

CLASS ACTIVITY

After students have read *Gorilla,* discuss the zoo in the book as well as other zoos they have visited. Talk about traditional zoos, where animals are kept in cages, and modern zoos, where animals live in natural habitats. Tell students they are going to create their own modern zoo. Ask students to bring in any stuffed animal they wish and then decide which animals they think would be happy living together. Have students work together to create a "natural environment" for their animals. They can use paper, clay, toys, and other materials to create their zoo. They may wish to design real environments such as an African plain or make imaginary places. When all the exhibits are finished, invite others to visit.

NAME ______________________ DATE ____________

A Visit to the Zoo

Hannah visits the zoo to see the gorilla. There are many other animals that live in the zoo. Draw a picture of your favorite zoo animal. Then write a sentence about why you like the animal. If you wish, write another sentence about what you would like to do with the animal.

____

____

____

Hawk, I'm Your Brother

BYRD BAYLOR
(NEW YORK: CHARLES SCRIBNER'S SONS, 1976)

ALL ABOUT THE BOOK

In *Hawk, I'm Your Brother,* Rudy Soto, a young Native American boy, dreams of flying. He steals and cares for a young hawk, but soon realizes that the bird must be set free. Once he lets the bird go, Rudy is able to feel the joy of flight as the hawk soars through the sky.

CLASS ACTIVITY

Have students imagine that Rudy did *not* set the hawk free. How might the story have been different? With this change in mind, have students work in small groups to come up with alternate endings to the book. After students discuss their new endings, have one person in the group act as a recorder, writing down the new ending. Ask each group to share their ending with the class. Ask the class to decide which ending—including the original—seems most suitable. Explore with students the reasons for their choice.

NAME ______________________________ DATE ______________

My Side of the Story

Writing as Rudy, explain in your journal why you took the hawk. To help you get started, list three reasons for your actions.

My reasons for taking the bird:

1. ______________________

2. ______________________

3. ______________________

My journal entry:

____

____

____

____

____

____

____

____

Hershel and the Hanukkah Goblins

ERIC KIMMEL
ILLUSTRATED BY TRINA SCHART HAYMAN
(NEW YORK: HOLIDAY HOUSE, 1989)

ALL ABOUT THE BOOK

Hershel and the Hanukkah Goblins is about Hershel of Ostropol. As he walks to the next village, Hershel eagerly anticipates the bright candles, merry songs, and potato pancakes of Hanukkah that wait for him. But when he arrives, he discovers that the villagers are too frightened of the goblins that haunt the old synagogue to celebrate Hanukkah. Hershel outwits the goblins by winning at dreidel and using various other clever ideas. The synagogue is destroyed, but the menorah remains and the villagers rejoice. This book was a Caldecott Honor Book for 1990.

CLASS ACTIVITY

Bring in some dreidels and raisins, nuts, or small candies. Spin the square-shaped tops and point out the Hebrew letters *nun, gimel, hay,* and *shin* on the sides. The letters spell out *Nes Gadol Hayah Sham,* meaning "A Great Miracle Happened There," referring to the Jewish defeat of the Syrian army in 164 B.C. Then teach students how to play dreidel, the game Hershel used to defeat one of the goblins. Give each student an equal share of the pot. The game starts when players each put a piece into the middle and one player spins the top. If *nun* comes up, the spinner gets nothing; *gimel,* the pot; *hay,* half; *shin,* the spinner adds a piece to the pot. The game is over when one person wins. The winner is the first one to obtain the whole pot and every other player's share of goodies.

Remind students that Hershel made up his own version of the game to defeat the goblin. Then challenge small groups of children to create their own set of rules for playing dreidel, keeping fairness in mind. Group members work together to write their rules or illustrate how to play. When the groups are finished, they share their rules and the class tries the new versions to see if the rules make sense and are fair.

NAME ____________________ DATE ____________

Celebrate!

Hershel and the Hanukkah Goblins celebrates freedom. Other holidays celebrate different things. Pick your favorite holiday and tell about what it celebrates. Describe what you and your family do on this holiday. Explain why it is your favorite.

Hey, Al

ARTHUR YORINKS
ILLUSTRATED BY RICHARD EGIELSKI
(NEW YORK: FARRAR, STRAUS AND GIROUX, 1986)

ALL ABOUT THE BOOK

Hey, Al tells about Al and his dog, Eddie, who are dissatisfied with everything in their lives. When a bird takes them to an island in the sky, they are delighted, until they realize that staying on the island means they will change into birds. They soon learn to appreciate home. The book received the Caldecott Medal in 1987.

CLASS ACTIVITY

Al and Eddie travel to an island in the sky. Have students imagine that they are in Al's place on the island. Then have them write postcards to a relative or friend back home, explaining what they see and their feelings about the experience. On the other side of the card, have students draw a picture of what they see on the island.

NAME ______________________ DATE ______________

If I Were a . . .

Al and Eddie almost turn into birds. How would you feel as a bird? Answer these questions to put yourself in Al's place.

1. If I were a bird, I would be a ______________________

because ______________________.

2. If I were a color, I would be ______________________

because ______________________.

3. If I were a place, I would be ______________________

because ______________________.

4. If I were a tree, I would be a ______________________

because ______________________.

5. If I were a tool, I would be a ______________________

because ______________________.

Jumanji

CHRIS VAN ALLSBURG
(BOSTON: HOUGHTON MIFFLIN, 1981)

ALL ABOUT THE BOOK

In *Jumanji,* Peter and Judy start a new game that must be played until one player reaches "the golden city." After the first roll of the dice, the game comes alive. Wild animals appear, monsoons rain down, and volcanoes erupt. Judy reaches the golden city just in time to have the house and game return to normal as their parents come home. The book received the Caldecott Medal in 1982.

CLASS ACTIVITY

Have pairs of students design their own board game. Suggest they begin by deciding on the game's theme, such as the Wild West, African Safari, or Space World. Next, have them establish and record the rules, reviewing those in Jumanji for suggestions. Students then make the game board and the playing pieces. When everyone is finished, encourage children to share their games and to play as many of their classmates' games as possible.

NAME ______________________ DATE ____________

Play the Game

Each of these five game pieces tells about something that happened in *Jumanji*. Cut out the game pieces and arrange them on the game board in the correct order from one to five. Then read the pieces in order to see if the steps make sense.

Wild animals appear and a volcano erupts.

Judy reaches the golden city.

The game returns to normal.

The game comes alive.

Peter and Judy's parents leave.

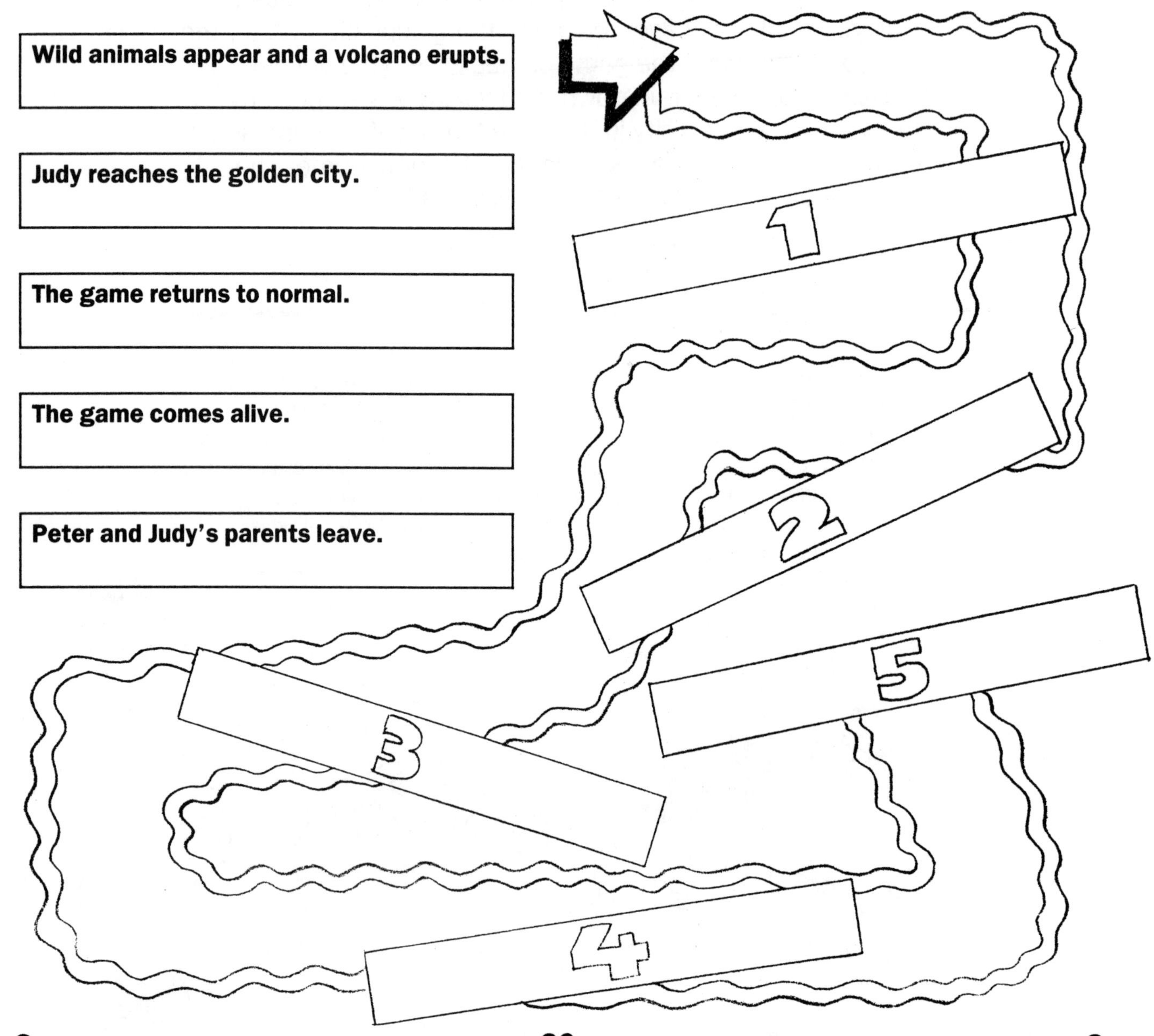

Lon Po Po:

A RED RIDING HOOD STORY FROM CHINA

ED YOUNG
(NEW YORK: PHILOMEL BOOKS, 1989)

ALL ABOUT THE BOOK

Lon Po Po: A Red Riding Hood Story From China takes place in ancient China, where a good woman lived with her three daughters, Shang, Tao, and Paotze. When the good woman leaves the children to visit their grandmother, whom they call Po Po, a wolf disguises himself as their granny and says he missed their mother along the way. Realizing the wolf's subterfuge, the oldest girl tricks the wolf into letting all three girls leave the house to pick gingko nuts for him to eat. The wolf calls to them. Pretending to share the nuts, the girls pull the wolf in a basket up to the top of the tree. At the last moment, they let the wolf crash to the ground, killing him and saving themselves. This book won the 1990 Caldecott Medal.

CLASS ACTIVITY

Lon Po Po is a Chinese version of the Little Red Riding Hood story. After students finish reading *Lon Po Po,* share *Little Red Riding Hood* with them. As a class, create a chart showing the differences and similarities between the two versions of the same folk tale. In both books, for example, the children are left alone and the wolf disguises himself as Granny. The gingko nuts, however, are unique to *Lon Po Po.* Display the chart for students to review and compare.

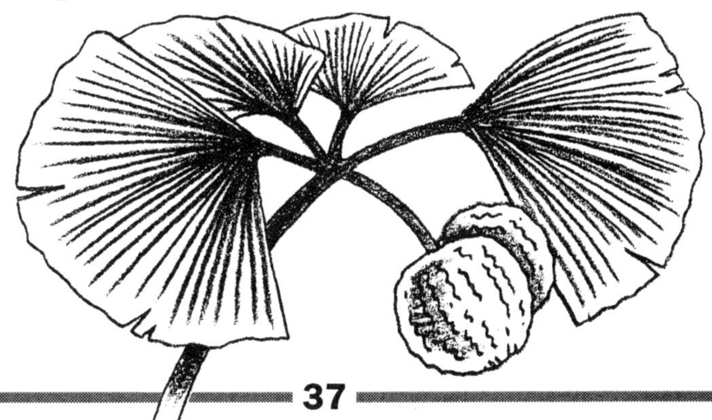

NAME ______________________________ DATE ______________

What a Problem!

The girls in *Lon Po Po* have quite a problem to solve! How would *you* solve each of these problems? Write your answers on the lines under each problem.

1. The person next to you copies from your math paper during a test. You know the person will fail math if he or she fails this test. What do you do? ______________________

____

2. Walking home from school on a snowy day, you find a skinny, homeless cat under a bush. You already have a pet. What do you do? ______________________

____

3. You borrow your sister's new sweater without asking. During recess, you tear the sleeve on the fence. What do you do? ______________________

____

4. You introduce a new student to your best friend. Suddenly, they are best friends and you're left out. What do you do? ______________________

____

A New Coat for Anna

HARRIET ZIEFERT
ILLUSTRATED BY ANITA LOBEL
(NEW YORK: ALFRED A. KNOPF, 1986)

ALL ABOUT THE BOOK

A New Coat for Anna takes place in the aftermath of World War II, and Anna's mother must make sacrifices to have a much-needed new coat made for Anna. She trades Grandfather's gold watch to get the wool, a lamp to have the wool spun, a garnet necklace to have it woven, and a teapot to have it sewn. The process takes a year, and Anna comes to know everyone involved in making her coat.

CLASS ACTIVITY

Have students write a brief critical review of *A New Coat for Anna.* First establish the criteria students will use. They may want to evaluate the characters, the story, or the pictures, for example. Then cut out coat shapes from different colors of construction paper and have students write their reviews on these shapes. A sample review might read: "I liked the book because it told about how hard it was for Anna's mother to get Anna a new coat. I also liked to see all the steps in making the coat." Display the coat-shaped reviews on a bulletin board.

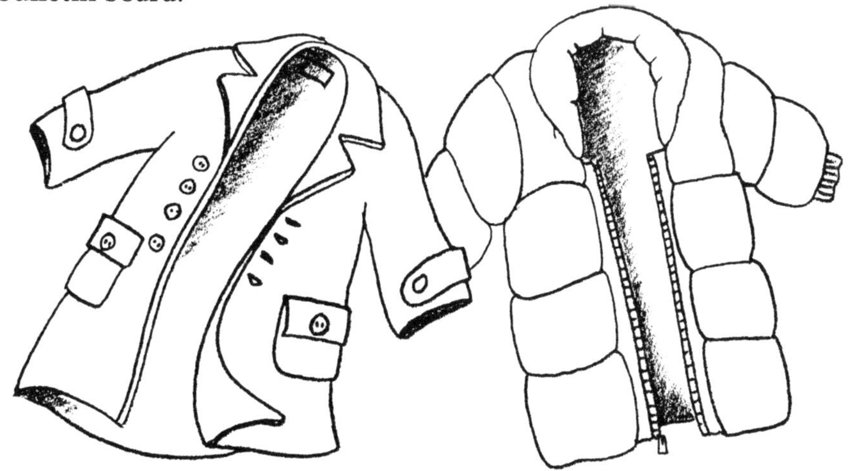

NAME ____________________ DATE ____________

Thank You

Anna is very happy with her new coat. Imagine that you are Anna. Write a thank-you note to your mother, telling why you like the coat so much. Before you begin, think about the sacrifices Anna's mother made for her.

No Star Nights

ANNA EGAN SMUCKER
(NEW YORK: ALFRED A. KNOPF, 1989)

ALL ABOUT THE BOOK

No Star Nights recounts the narrator's childhood as the daughter of a steelworker. Among her pleasures are her mother's stuffed cabbage, summer trips to Pittsburgh to see Pirates games at Forbes Field, and July when the workers get their vacation pay. Ash from the factory permeates all, even the nuns' starched white wimples. All night long the sky glows red, obscuring the stars. This book became an American Library Association Notable Book and a Notable Children's Trade Book in the Field of Social Studies, and won the International Reading Association Children's Book Award.

CLASS ACTIVITY

Encourage each student to select a character from the book. Using the book as a reference, ask students to list their character's personality traits. Then arrange students in pairs of different characters. Challenge student pairs to create a skit showing an adventure between their characters. After students practice their improvisations, ask them to perform their skits for the class.

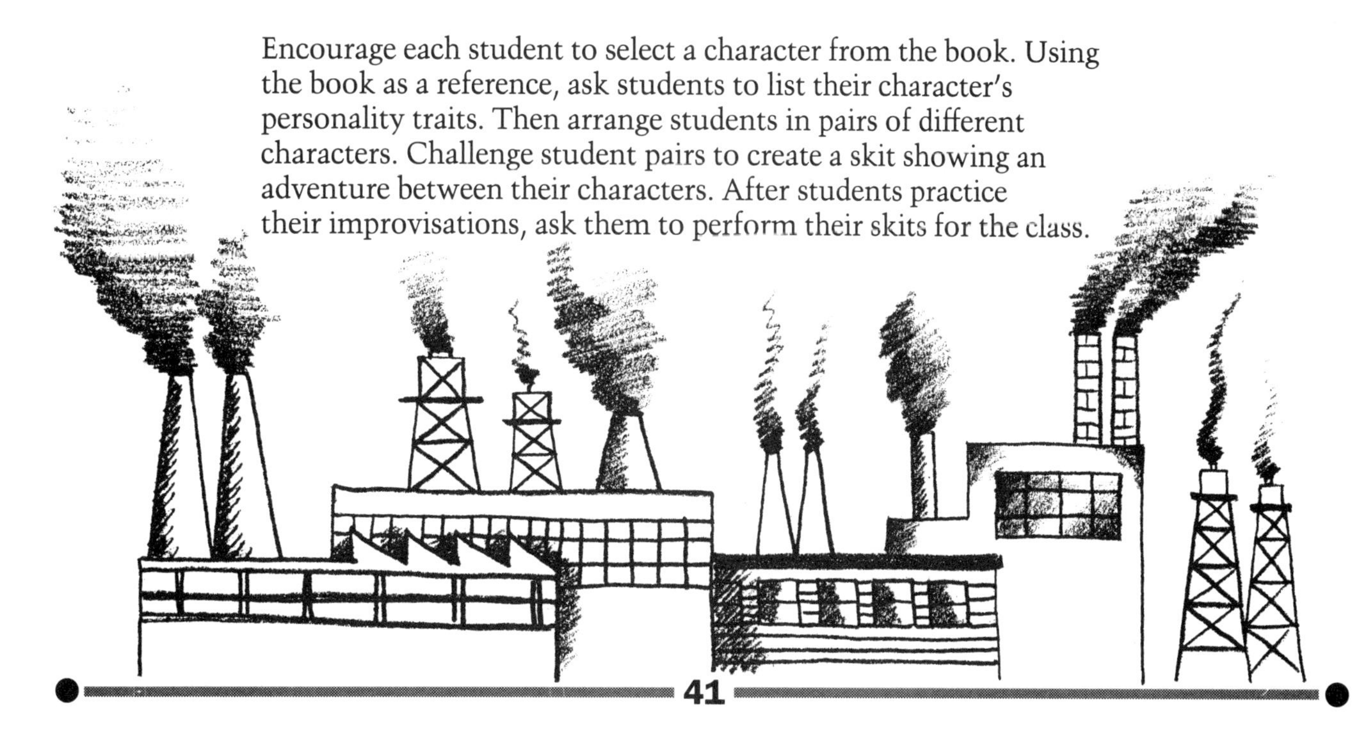

NAME ______________________ DATE ______________

Summertime Book

No Star Nights tells about things the author did when she was a child. Her favorite time was summer, when her father got his vacation pay and the family went to baseball games in Pittsburgh. Create a book about your own life. In each square, draw a picture of something you like to do during the summer and describe it on the lines. Then cut the squares apart. Staple them together to make your book.

Shake My Sillies Out

RAFFI
(NEW YORK: CROWN PUBLISHERS, 1987)

ALL ABOUT THE BOOK

Shake My Sillies Out contains five stanzas of a joyous song that show how to "shake sillies out," "wiggle waggles away," "clap crazies out," "jump jiggles out," and "yawn sleepies out." The song has been recorded by the popular children's singer, Raffi, on Troubadour Records (distributed through A & M Records, Hollywood, CA 90028).

CLASS ACTIVITY

Have children stand up and repeat the lyrics as they "shake their sillies out," "wiggle their waggles out," and so on. Then arrange students in small groups and invite them to create additional stanzas. Point out the alliteration (shake/sillies, wiggle/waggles, clap/crazies, jump/jiggles) and encourage them to try to find words that share the same initial sound. After the groups create their stanzas, have the class try them on for size!

NAME ______________________ DATE ____________

Shake My Sillies Out!

In the five squares below, draw a cartoon showing people acting out this book. Under each square, write a sentence that tells what part of the song they are doing.

Sunken Treasure

GAIL GIBBONS
(NEW YORK: THOMAS Y. CROWELL, 1988)

ALL ABOUT THE BOOK

To show how modern treasure hunters do their work, *Sunken Treasure* focuses on the search for the wreck of the seventeenth-century Spanish galleon *Neustra Señora de Atocha.* The *Atocha*'s cargo is one of the richest such treasures ever found. The importance of this discovery—and others like it—goes beyond the monetary worth of the galleon's treasure. Modern treasure hunters bring bits of history to the surface, and this look at the past makes a treasure priceless.

CLASS ACTIVITY

Ask students to imagine that they are on a treasure hunt and that they have found astonishing riches at the bottom of the ocean. They have very little time to report their findings, however, as they must salvage the treasure quickly, before the summer storms come. Challenge students to write brief telegrams or faxes describing what they found in twenty-five words or fewer. The purpose of their communication is to alert the media to their findings, so their transmissions must be complete yet concise.

NAME ________________________________ DATE ______________

Treasure!

Imagine that *you* found an old pirate treasure map. What would it look like? Draw the treasure map below. Include drawings and labels for landmarks such as reefs, sunken ships, and underwater caves. Be sure to put an X on the spot where the treasure can be found! Then write a sentence telling what you plan to do with your findings.

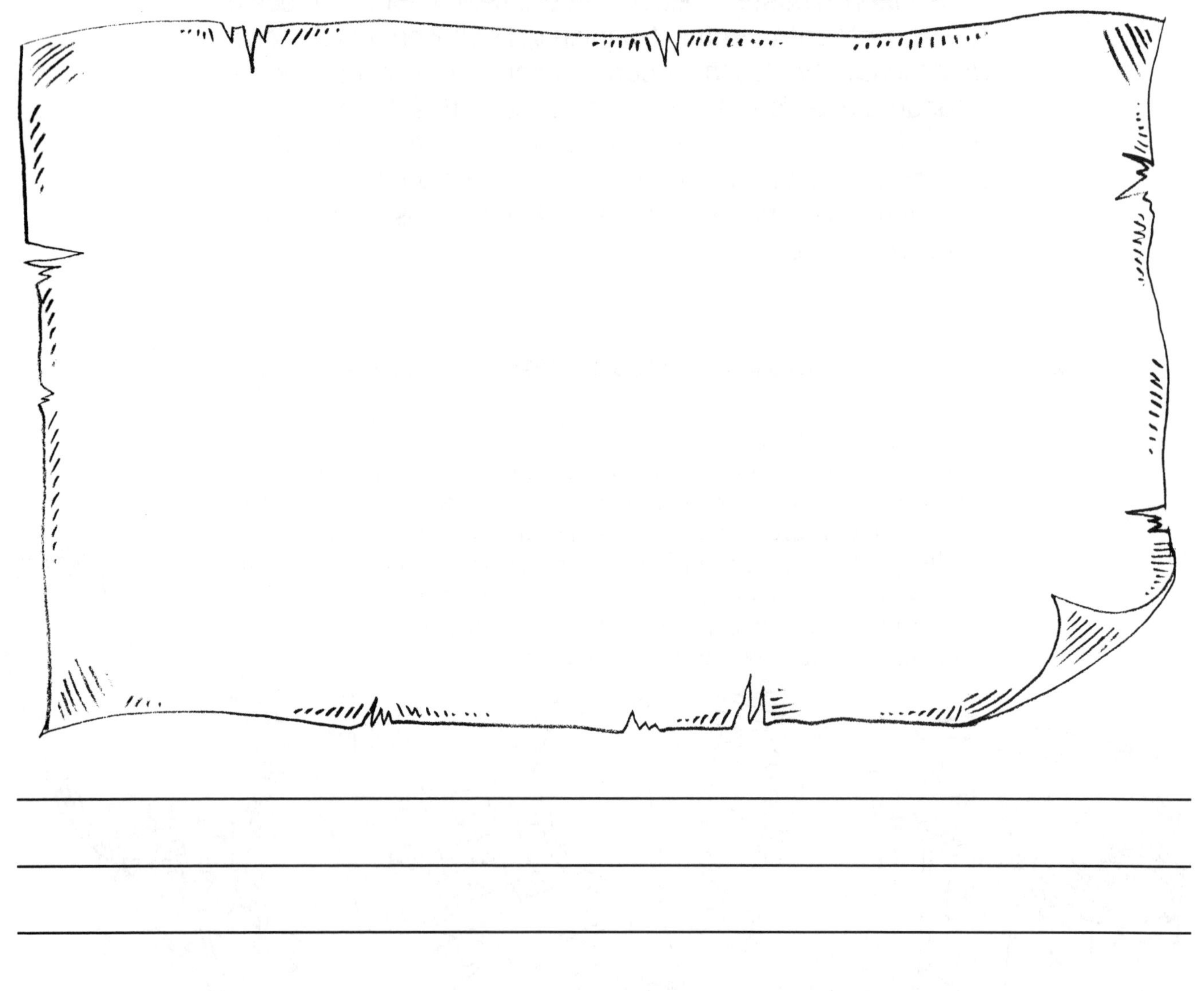

____

____

____

____

Truck

DONALD CREWS
(NEW YORK: GREENWILLOW BOOKS, 1980)

ALL ABOUT THE BOOK

Truck, a Caldecott Honor book, is a picture book that gives children the opportunity to make their own story. Road signs and the writing on the trucks are the only words provided in this book. Readers can use their own words to describe the journeys of trucks that carry various goods.

CLASS ACTIVITY

Ask students to look through magazines and newspapers to find pictures of different kinds of trucks. Collect all the pictures and distribute four or five to everyone. Then have students paste the truck pictures on poster-sized pieces of paper and write a few simple words to create a story, telling what the trucks are carrying, where they come from, and where they are going. Collect all the pages and create a class truck big book. Encourage each student to read his or her page to the class. Display the big book for students to enjoy again and again.

NAME ________________________________ DATE ______________

Go, Truck, Go!

Under each truck, write a sentence that tells where you think it is going.

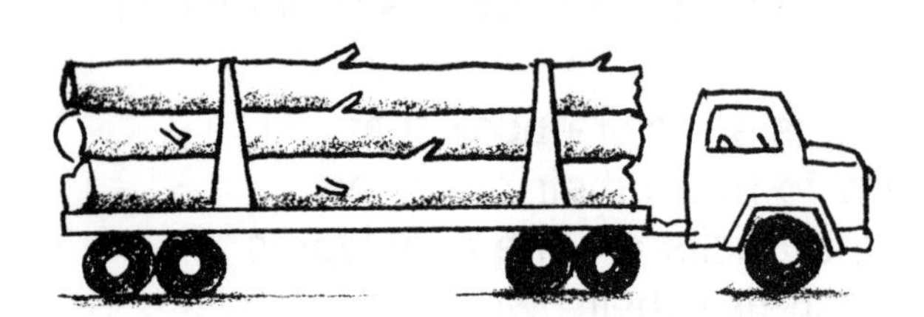

______________________________ ______________________________

______________________________ ______________________________

______________________________ ______________________________

The Wednesday Surprise

EVE BUNTING
ILLUSTRATED BY DONALD CARRICK
(BOSTON: HOUGHTON MIFFLIN, 1990)

ALL ABOUT THE BOOK

In *The Wednesday Surprise,* Grandma comes to Anna's house on Wednesday nights with a big bag of books. Together they read many stories and plan a surprise for Dad's birthday. Finally, one Saturday his birthday arrives and the family gathers. Just when Dad thinks he has received all his presents, Anna gives him the Wednesday surprise, revealing that Anna has taught Grandma to read.

CLASS ACTIVITY

Arrange the class into small groups. Give each group a very simple story they can memorize (paraphrasing, if necessary). Have groups meet for a brief time daily until everyone has memorized the assigned story. Then have individuals tell their story to the class, to members of another group, or to younger schoolmates. Urge students to vary the inflection of their voices to create drama and keep their audience attentive and excited.

NAME ______________________________ DATE ______________

My Library

Grandma and Anna have many favorite books. What books do you like best? Name six books you like a lot. After the title of the book, write one sentence to explain why you like it.

1. ______________________________

   ____

2. ______________________________

   ____

3. ______________________________

   ____

4. ______________________________

   ____

5. ______________________________

   ____

6. ______________________________

   ____

Wilfrid Gordon McDonald Partridge

MEM FOX
ILLUSTRATED BY JULIE VIVAS
(NEW YORK: KANE/MILLER, 1985)

ALL ABOUT THE BOOK

Wilfrid Gordon McDonald Partridge enjoys being with the elderly people who live in the residence next door to his home. To help his favorite resident, Miss Nancy Alison Delacourt Cooper, recapture her failing memory, he asks his elderly friends for definitions of "memory." He then finds an object that expresses each of their definitions. Wilfrid presents his collection to Miss Nancy, which helps her "find" her lost memory. Together they share special personal times.

CLASS ACTIVITY

Wilfrid Gordon McDonald Partridge describes a positive relationship between the generations. Have students select an elderly person such as a relative, family friend, or neighbor to interview. Have the class first work together to create a list of ten questions to ask the person. Questions might include "When you were my age, how was school different from now?" and "What did you do in your spare time?" During the interview, students can record the answers in their notebooks or use a tape recorder. Students might want to ask the people they interview for pictures of themselves as children. When everyone has completed the project, play the tapes or have students read their written interviews for the class to share. After students have listened to the interviews, encourage them to discuss what they have learned about the older generation and what they can do to bring the generations closer together.

NAME ______________________________ DATE ____________

My Memories

Wilfrid Gordon McDonald Partridge helps Miss Nancy remember special times in her life by making a collection of objects that would "find" her memory. What objects help you remember special times?

Make your own memory collection. Think of four objects that help you remember special times. In each box below, draw a picture of one object. Then write about the memory each object holds for you.

Object 1

____

____

Object 2

____

____

Object 3

____

____

Object 4

____

____

. . . and now Miguel

JOSEPH KRUMGOLD
(NEW YORK: THOMAS Y. CROWELL, 1953)

ALL ABOUT THE BOOK

. . . and now Miguel tells about twelve-year-old Miguel Chavez, who yearns to accompany the men of his family to the Sangre de Cristo Mountains, where they take their sheep to graze during the summer. Miguel works hard on the family sheep farm near Taos, New Mexico, and prays for the chance to be considered mature enough to go with the men during the summer. He gets his wish when his adored older brother, Gabriel, is drafted into the army. Although Miguel is sad his brother must leave, he is thrilled for the chance to help herd the sheep and the coming of age it represents. This book won the 1954 Newbery Medal.

CLASS ACTIVITY

Explain to students that sheep have been useful to people for a very long time—the animals were domesticated more than 10,000 years ago in the Middle East. The average sheep is about five feet (1½ m) long, weighs 150 to 350 pounds (67 to 157 kg), and can live as long as 13 years. The leading sheep-raising countries, in descending order, are Australia, the USSR, China, New Zealand, India, Turkey, Iran, the United States, and Pakistan. In America, sheep are raised primarily in Texas, Wyoming, Claifornia, South Dakota, and New Mexico. Write the word *sheep* in the middle of the chalkboard and make a semantic map or web by asking students to list all the things sheep contribute to our lives. Suggestions might include wool for clothing and furnishings, meat (lamb and mutton), and milk for drinking and cheesemaking.

NAME ______________________ DATE ____________

. . . and more Miguel

At the end of *. . . and now Miguel,* Miguel Chavez goes with the men of his family to the Sangre de Cristo Mountains, where they graze the sheep for the summer. What do you think happens to Miguel next? Take up Miguel's story after he returns home in the fall. How has he changed? On the lines below, write the next chapter in Miguel's life.

Charlotte's Web

E.B. WHITE
ILLUSTRATED BY GARTH WILLIAMS
(NEW YORK: HARPER & ROW, 1952)

ALL ABOUT THE BOOK

In *Charlotte's Web,* Wilbur, a runt pig, is lovingly raised by a girl named Fern. But once Wilbur grows, her parents make Fern sell the pig to her uncle, Mr. Zuckerman, who plans to sell Wilbur for his meat. In Mr. Zuckerman's barn, Wilbur meets Charlotte the spider, as well as other farm animals. Charlotte succeeds in saving Wilbur's life by writing in her web "terrific," "some pig," and other messages describing his virtues.

CLASS ACTIVITY

Templeton the Rat amasses a collection of objects he treasures. Discuss with students how people also collect things. Explore the different things people collect, such as coins, stamps, baseball cards, comic books, and records. Then ask students to put together their own collections of things they value. The collections do not have to be on a single theme; students might include such diverse objects as marbles, pictures, and postcards. Have students share their collections with the class and discuss how their collections are the same as or different from Templeton's.

NAME ______________________________ DATE ______________

Help Wilbur!

Charlotte the spider saves Wilbur's life by writing different words that describe his good qualities in her web. How would *you* go about saving Wilbur? Design a completely new way to save poor Wilbur from becoming bacon. Write your ideas on the lines below.

____

____

____

____

____

____

____

____

____

____

Dear Mr. Henshaw

BEVERLY CLEARY
(NEW YORK: WILLIAM MORROW, 1983)

ALL ABOUT THE BOOK

Dear Mr. Henshaw describes how Leigh Botts comes to terms with being the new kid in school, with the disappearance of his dog Bandit, and most important, with his parents' divorce. One way he expresses his feelings is by writing to his favorite author, Mr. Henshaw, and keeping a diary. This book won the 1984 Newbery Medal.

CLASS ACTIVITY

Leigh Botts successfully rigs a burglar alarm in his lunch box to stop thieves from stealing his lunch. Suggest that students create and build their own unique inventions. Direct students to begin by deciding on the purpose of their invention. Then have them fashion their inventions from commonplace materials such as cardboard boxes, paper, string, cardboard tubes, and found objects. More advanced students might want to use batteries to power their creations. When all students have completed their work, have them write brief descriptions of their inventions' purpose and function. Then gather all the inventions for display and ask each student to read his or her description to the class, demonstrating how the invention works.

NAME ______________________________ DATE ______________

Take a Letter!

Leigh Botts writes letters to his favorite author, Mr. Henshaw. On the lines below, write a letter to an author you greatly admire. In your letter, explain why you admire his or her work. Talk about specific books by this author that you have read and include some of the details from these books that you liked.

Dear ____________________:

Hailstones and Halibut Bones: Adventures in Color

MARY O'NEILL
(NEW YORK: DOUBLEDAY, 1973)

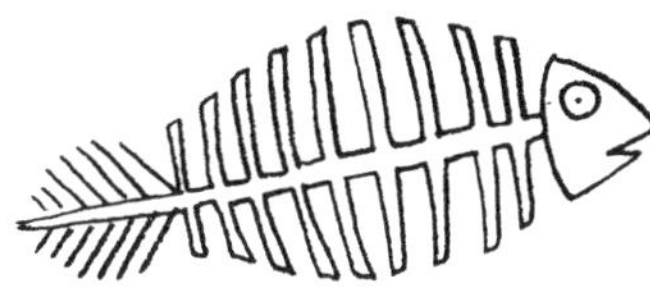

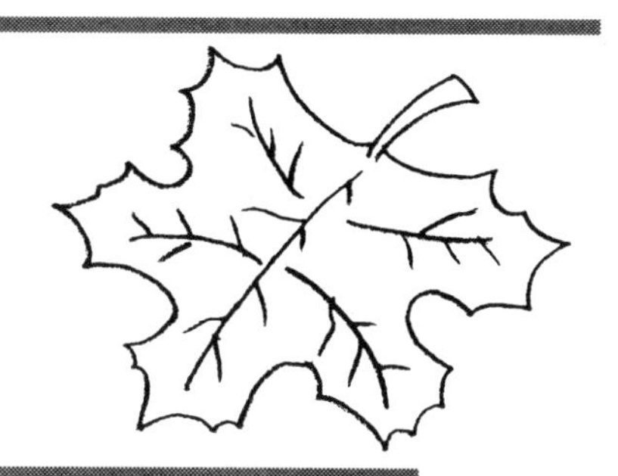

ALL ABOUT THE BOOK

Hailstones and Halibut Bones: Adventures in Color is a collection of highly imaginative poems, each about a different color: purple, gold, black, brown, blue, gray, white, orange, red, pink, green, yellow. Each poem expresses the author's various feelings about colors and in so doing captures both the ordinary and extraordinary meaning of color.

CLASS ACTIVITY

Since *Hailstones and Halibut Bones: Adventures in Color* is a collection of poems, suggest that students try their own hands at writing a poem. Begin by having them select a subject they would like to write about, such as their pet, an experience, a feeling, a place, or a person. Explain that their poems can rhyme if they wish, but that they need not. These are going to be special poems, though, in that each line is going to have only two words in it. Here's a sample:

Summer night
Fireflies light
Children laugh
We play
Balls fly
Bicycles zoom
Parents talk
Trees sway

Give students time to write their poems. Then have them share their efforts by gathering all the poems into a class book.

NAME ______________________________ DATE ______________

Making Comparisons

In *Hailstones and Halibut Bones: Adventures in Color,* Mary O'Neill explains what different colors are like by comparing them to concrete objects. She compares white, for example, to snow and to light. When these comparisons use the words *like* or *as,* they are called *similes.* Writers use similes to help readers form vivid mental images of ideas.

Complete each of the six phrases below to create fresh, new similes.

1. The rose is as red as ______________________________.
2. She rushed through the doorway like ______________________________.
3. The wind is as cold as ______________________________.
4. The movie was so sad that they cried like ______________________________.
5. The meat is as tender as ______________________________.
6. The waves sparkle like ______________________________.

Hatchet

GARY PAULSEN
(NEW YORK: PENGUIN, 1988)

ALL ABOUT THE BOOK

Brian Robeson is the lone survivor of an airplane crash in the Canadian wilderness. For 54 days Brian struggles to survive, armed with only a small hatchet and his wits. After his initial panic and despair, Brian succeeds in building a shelter, crafting hunting tools, and finding food. He is rescued when a passing pilot picks up the signal from the emergency transmitter Brian had just salvaged from the wreck of the downed airplane. *Hatchet* was a Newbery Honor Book in 1988.

CLASS ACTIVITY

Brian survives in the Canadian wilderness because he realizes the different ways he can use his small hatchet—to fell wood for a shelter, to shave slivers of bark to ignite a spark of fire, to whittle sticks to use to catch fish. Challenge students to choose an item from the following list and brainstorm as many ways as they can to use the items. Students can work individually, in teams, or as a class.

- a piece of paper
- a blanket
- a pillow
- a book
- a screw
- a cup
- a wooden block
- a metal nail file

NAME ______________________________ DATE ____________

Write It Yourself

In *Hatchet,* Brian must use his wits to survive in what at first seems to him a hopeless situation. As it turns out, Brian has the adventure of a lifetime, which affects him the rest of his life. Now write your own adventure story about a character or characters you create. Read the plan below to help you get started.

1. Invent one or two main characters and give them names. Decide what they look like and what kinds of personalities they have.
2. Pick a setting for your story. Describe it in words that tell how it looks, smells, and sounds.
3. Create an adventurous situation for your character(s). Think about danger and excitement.
4. Think about how your character(s) feel and how their feelings change.
5. Choose a way for your character(s) to resolve the situation.
6. Make sure your ending connects any loose ends in your story.

Write the first draft of your story below and on the back of this paper. Use additional paper if you need to. Then write your final copy on fresh paper and share your story with a classmate.

____

____

____

____

Island of the Blue Dolphins

SCOTT O'DELL
(BOSTON: HOUGHTON MIFFLIN, 1960)

ALL ABOUT THE BOOK

Island of the Blue Dolphins, set in the early 1800s, is based on a true story. Beset by Aleutian tribes hunting sea otters, the Indians of San Nicolas Island sail to another island. Karana jumps overboard to return to her younger brother, who was accidentally left on shore. When her brother dies soon after being attacked by a pack of ferocious wild dogs, Karana is left alone on the island. She spends eighteen years alone, safeguarding her precarious food supply, battling the elements, and guarding against the return of the Aleutians. Her quiet courage, self-reliance, and acceptance of her fate are inspirational. This book won the 1961 Newbery Medal.

CLASS ACTIVITY

Dolphins play a very important role in the novel. In the beginning, for example, their cheerful presence sustains Karana on her perilous canoe ride back to the island. Have students research dolphins and present their findings to the class in the form of panel discussions. Begin by dividing the class into small groups. Assign each group one aspect of the topic, such as what the personalities of different species are like, physical descriptions, what they eat, their behavior, intelligence, and vocalization. Students can consult encyclopedias, books on the subject, and magazine articles for information. Suggest that students illustrate their presentations with pictures of dolphins. Interested students can work together to write a summary of the information presented.

NAME ______________________ DATE __________

Survival!

Alone on San Nicolas Island, Karana survives on the roots she can dig up, the berries she can gather, and the fish she can spear. She has only very basic tools: a bow and arrows, rocks, and bone knives. When she is very thirsty and unable to reach the spring of clear water, she sucks on a cactus leaf.

Imagine that *you* are shipwrecked on a desert island. How would you use the things you have in your pockets and backpack or schoolbag to survive? In the space below, list the ways you could use the things you have with you. Then describe five more items you wish you had and how you could use them to help you survive.

How I will use the things I brought with me to survive:

____

____

____

____

____

____

Five more items I wish I had brought with me and how I would use them:

1. ______________________
2. ______________________
3. ______________________
4. ______________________
5. ______________________

Dicey's Song

CYNTHIA VOIGT
(NEW YORK: FAWCETT JUNIPER, 1982)

ALL ABOUT THE BOOK

Family relationships. Responsibility. Bravery. Courage. These are the themes that emerge in Cynthia Voigt's young adult novel, *Dicey's Song.*

Their mother hospitalized, Dicey and her younger brothers and sister go to live with the grandmother they have never known. While there, the family learns their strengths and weaknesses. Dicey makes a friend in her new school and realizes that others have personal struggles, too. After a painful trip with Gran to visit Dicey's dying mother, she learns that, though life is rocky, and the road unsure, she has the strength and courage to remember the past while carving out a hopeful future.

Dicey's Song won the Newbery Medal in 1983.

CLASS ACTIVITY

Dicey's English teacher, Mr. Chappelle, asked his class what forms conflict can take in a story. Dicey thought of a conflict between a powerful person and a powerless person, between someone honest and someone dishonest, and even between someone and his (or her) self.

Explore with students the various conflicts in *Dicey's Song*. Ask children to work in cooperative learning groups to brainstorm and record conflicts they see *between* characters in the story (for example, between Dicey and her mother), and *within* a character (for example, those inside Dicey herself). Have the groups share their ideas with the class and discuss. Which conflict do the students see as most painful? the easiest to resolve?

NAME ______________________ DATE ____________

A Character Sketch

Dicey wrote a character sketch of someone she knew. You will write a sketch of a character in *Dicey's Song.*

Select a character from the story. Tell about the character in a way that makes him or her "come alive." You can give physical traits and behavioral traits, and explain why that character is memorable. You can also tell about conflicts the character faces.

A character sketch of ______________________.
(character's name)

Jacob Have I Loved

KATHERINE PATERSON
(NEW YORK: THOMAS Y. CROWELL, 1980)

ALL ABOUT THE BOOK

Set on the small windswept Rass Island in Chesapeake Bay during and immediately after World War II, the novel describes Louise Bradshaw's resentment over her beautiful and accomplished fraternal twin sister Caroline. As she sinks deeper into a life of bitterness and acrimony, Louise finally realizes she must help herself. She enters college on the mainland and comes into her own, eventually marrying and becoming a nurse-midwife. This book won the Newbery Medal in 1981.

CLASS ACTIVITY

Louise and Caroline are twins, yet are different in every respect. Suggest students research the topic of twins. Begin by arranging the class in small groups. Assign each group one aspect of the topic, or have students select their own subtopics. Possible subtopics include the different types of twins (fraternal and identical), the probability o twin births, and cell division. Then have students share their findings with the rest of the class in the form of an oral report. Where appropriate, suggest that students illustrate their presentations with original charts or pictures they found in their research. If you have a set of twins in your class, or a student who is brother or sister to a twin, encourage them to share with classmates the advantages or disadvantages of being a twin.

NAME ______________________________ DATE ______________

Same Difference

Louise and Caroline Bradshaw are twins, yet they are very different. On the lines below, list each girl's character traits. Look back through the book for passages that reveal their personalities. Then make a prediction about what the future holds for each girl after the story ends, based on her character traits.

Louise
Character Traits:

1. ______________
2. ______________
3. ______________
4. ______________
5. ______________
6. ______________

Prediction:

____
____
____

Caroline
Character Traits:

1. ______________
2. ______________
3. ______________
4. ______________
5. ______________
6. ______________

Prediction:

____
____
____

Julie of the Wolves

JEAN CRAIGHEAD GEORGE
(NEW YORK: HARPER & ROW, 1972)

ALL ABOUT THE BOOK

Julie of the Wolves, the 1973 Newbery Medal winner, describes how a young Eskimo woman, Julie Miyax Edwards, survives alone on the Alaskan tundra using her own intelligence and self-reliance.

CLASS ACTIVITY

Suggest that students design a book jacket for *Julie of the Wolves.* Remind students that an effective book jacket both attracts the reader's attention and conveys the content of the book. Then brainstorm with students the elements of a book jacket: the picture on the front, a brief summary on the inside, and perhaps quotations from the book or endorsements from reviews on the back. When students have completed their book jackets, create a display in a corner of the room.

NAME ______________________________ DATE ______________

I Need Advice!

Imagine that you are Julie Edwards. Review the problems that you face, especially your decision to run away from your husband, Daniel. Write a letter to an advice columnist, asking for ways to deal with your situation. Then write a response to the letter as though you were the advice columnist.

Dear Advice Columnist:

____

____

____

____

____

____

Signed,

Julie of the Wolves

Dear Julie of the Wolves:

____

____

____

____

____

____

Signed,

Advice Columnist

Maniac Magee

JERRY SPINELLI
(BOSTON: LITTLE, BROWN, 1990)

ALL ABOUT THE BOOK

Maniac Magee is about Jeffrey Lionel Magee, a white boy who is orphaned at age three when his parents are killed in a trolley accident. He is sent to live with his aunt and uncle in western Pennsylvania, but the couple is so bitterly estranged that Jeffrey runs away when he is eleven years old. He lives on the streets for a time, where his outstanding athletic ability and bravery earn him the nickname "Maniac." Jeffrey is taken in by the kindly Beales, a black family. He is happy living with them, until racial conflicts drive him away. For a time he lives with Grayson, an aged park attendant. After Grayson's death, Maniac lives with a bigoted white family, the McNabs. Maniac tries to bring about understanding between the races and eventually finds a home with the Beales. This book won the 1990 Boston Globe/Horn Book Award for fiction and the 1991 Newbery Medal.

CLASS ACTIVITY

The legend of Maniac Magee grows through oral repetition, as various stories of Jeffrey's bravery weave together. To demonstrate this process, challenge students to write cooperative stories. Arrange students in small groups. Ask one student in each group to write the beginning of a story, about a paragraph long. Students then pass their papers to the group member on their right, who writes another paragraph. Students continue this process until the story is finished. Then ask each group to take turns reading their stories aloud so that everyone can see how his or her contribution was woven into the story.

NAME ______________________________ DATE ______________

The Legend Lives On

Maniac Magee becomes a legend in part because of his outstanding athletic abilities, and also for his ability to show black and white people that they can be friends. Imagine you want to honor Maniac for his legendary achievements. You decide he should be in a Kids' Hall of Fame. Complete this form to nominate Maniac Magee for the Kids' Hall of Fame.

1. Name of person nominated: ______________________________

2. Outstanding plays in main sport or sports: ______________________________

____

3. Other outstanding achievements: ______________________________

____

____

____

4. Characters in *Maniac Magee* who would also want to nominate him: ______________

____

____

____

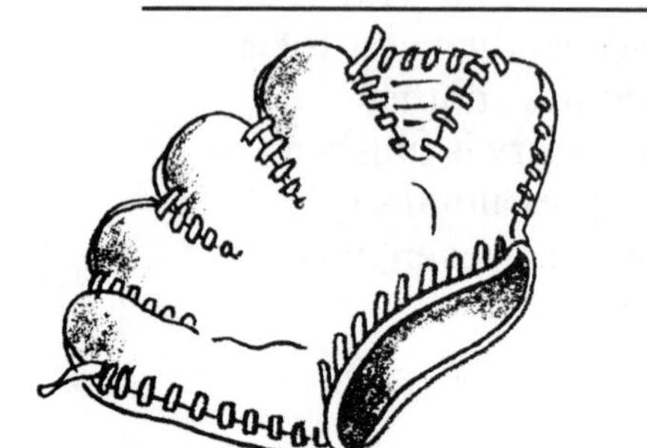

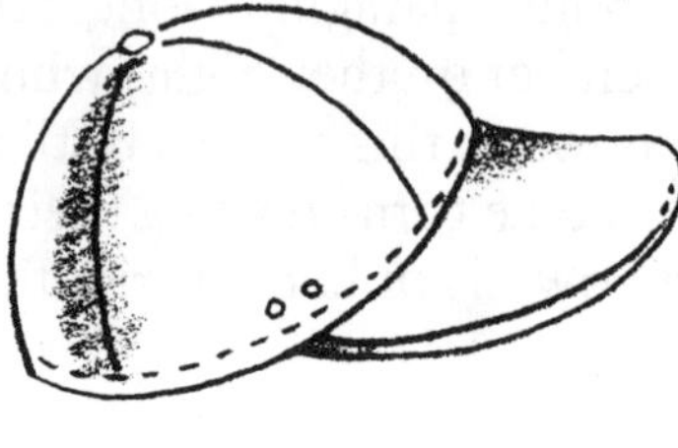

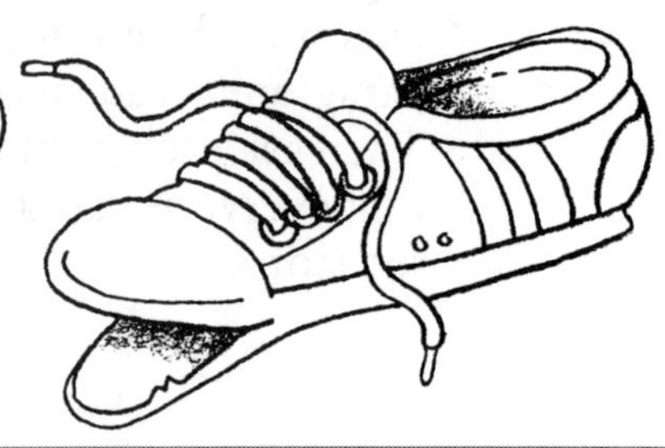

M. C. Higgins, the Great

VIRGINIA HAMILTON
(NEW YORK: MACMILLAN, 1974)

ALL ABOUT THE BOOK

M.C. *Higgins, the Great,* the 1975 Newbery Medal winner, describes an African-American family struggling to protect their home and environment from strip miners. At first, thirteen-year-old Mayo Cornelius Higgins, M.C., tries to get his family to leave their home on Sarah's Mountain because a strip-mining spoil heap threatens them with destruction. By the end of the novel, however, M.C. has come to see what Sarah's Mountain means to his family. The family stays and fights the menace by building a barrier wall.

CLASS ACTIVITY

The process of strip mining has been criticized for the serious damage it does to the environment. Ask students to imagine that they are M.C. and that they want to call attention to the problem by writing a letter to the editor of the local paper. Guide students first to outline the situation facing M.C. and his family and then to suggest specific solutions. When everyone has finished writing, post the letters on a bulletin board for all to share.

NAME ______________________________ DATE ______________

Congratulations!

M. C. Higgins, the Great won the Newbery Medal for the best children's book of 1975. Why do you think this book won the award? Write a press release announcing the award and explaining why you think the book was selected. To help you get started, first list six things about the book you especially liked. You might want to include a specific character, a setting, the theme, or dialogue, for example.

Things I liked in *M. C. Higgins, the Great:*

1. ______________________ 4. ______________________

2. ______________________ 5. ______________________

3. ______________________ 6. ______________________

Press Release:

Number the Stars

LOIS LOWRY
(BOSTON: HOUGHTON MIFFLIN, 1989)

ALL ABOUT THE BOOK

Number the Stars is about a ten-year-old Danish girl named Annemarie Johansen, who bravely helps shelter her Jewish friend, Ellen Rosen, from the Nazis during the German occupation. Annemarie's parents and her uncle Henrik help the Rosen family and many other Jewish people escape across the sea to Sweden. The Johansens become emblematic of the Danes' success in saving almost their entire Jewish population, nearly 7,000 people, from the Nazis. This book won the 1990 Newbery Medal.

CLASS ACTIVITY

On a world map, have students identify and locate all the countries that were involved in World War II. They may want to consult an encyclopedia or their social studies books. Focus on Denmark and have volunteers explain why Denmark would become part of the Nazi empire and Sweden would remain free. Then have students locate Sweden and trace possible routes the Johansens and other Resistance workers might have taken from Copenhagen to Sweden to shelter their Jewish citizens. Finally, suggest that students write a coded postcard the Rosens might have sent to the Johansens, assuring their friends of their safe arrival in Sweden.

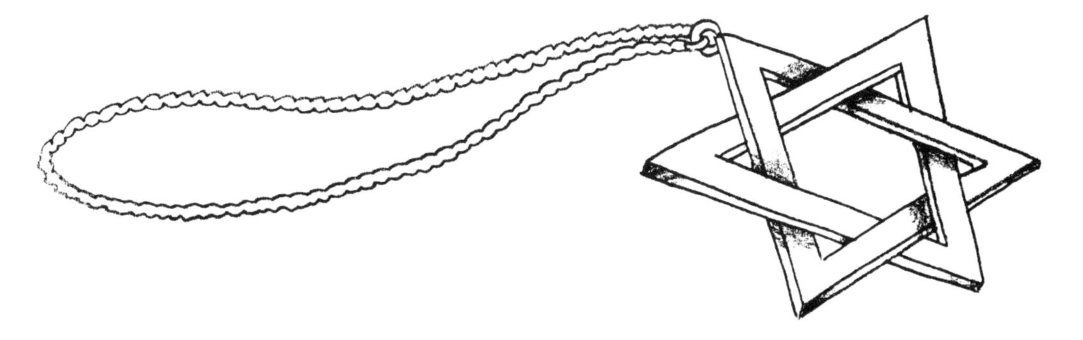

NAME ______________________________ DATE ______________

Peace on Earth

The United Nations has set aside the third Tuesday in September as the International Day of Peace. The actions of the Johansens and many of the Danes during World War II were one way to help further peace. People have suggested different ways for this day to be celebrated. What do *you* think?

First, decide how you think the United Nations International Day of Peace should be celebrated. Then, on the spaces below, write a letter to the editor of your local newspaper to convince readers to celebrate Peace Day as you recommend. Give specific reasons for your recommendation.

____

____

____

____

Dear ______________________________:

____

____

____

____

____

____

____

Yours very truly,

____

The Paper Crane

MOLLY BANG
(NEW YORK: GREENWILLOW BOOKS, 1985)

ALL ABOUT THE BOOK

In *The Paper Crane,* a restaurant owner can no longer make a living because a newly built highway now bypasses his restaurant. Despite his poverty, the restaurant owner gives a poor stranger a feast. The stranger pays with a folded paper crane that comes to life. The restaurant owner's business is restored when people flock to his eatery to see the magical dancing crane. Months later, the stranger returns and plays his flute. The crane flies away with the stranger on his back, but guests continue to frequent the restaurant to eat and hear the story of the gentle stranger and the magic paper crane. This is an ALA Notable Book and winner of the Boston Globe/Horn Book Award for illustration.

CLASS ACTIVITY

Explain to the class that paper folding is a very old art. In Japan, where it is called origami, paper folding is considered an art form. People skilled in origami can fold paper to create intricate birds, animals, fish, flowers, and even human figures. Introduce students to origami by having them fold paper to create simple objects such as airplanes, hats, and cups. If you wish to create more involved objects, consult an introduction to the technique, found in *Easy Origami* by Dokhuihtei Nakano (New York: Viking, 1986) and *Paper Pandas and Jumping Frogs* by Florence Temko (San Francisco: China Books, 1986).

NAME ______________________________ DATE ______________

What Does It Stand For?

In *The Paper Crane,* the crane brings good luck to the restaurant owner. The crane is a symbol, a concrete object that stands for an idea. In this case, the idea is good luck. Authors sometimes create personal symbols that have meaning for them. Other symbols are widely known to many people. An olive branch, for example, is a symbol of peace. A white flag symbolizes surrender. The crane is known throughout Asia as a symbol of good luck and long life.

Write a sentence to explain what each of these common symbols mean to you.

a dove

____

____

an eagle

____

____

a heart

____

____

a red rose

____

____

a fox

____

____

an owl

____

____

Rabbit Hill

ROBERT LAWSON
(NEW YORK: VIKING, 1944)

ALL ABOUT THE BOOK

Rabbit Hill is the story of the rabbits' and other animals' great rejoicing when they hear that "New Folks" are coming to live in the big empty farmhouse on Rabbit Hill. The rabbits are delighted because the coming of people means that a garden will be planted, which means there will be much food. Their hopes are rewarded, for not only is the garden big enough to provide for all, but the New Folks are more than happy to share its produce with the animals. The book received the Newbery Medal in 1945.

CLASS ACTIVITY

The quiet humor in this kindly tale makes it a good choice for a read-aloud event in the school or community. Divide the book into equal sections, one for each student. Working with a partner, have students practice reading their sections aloud. Encourage them to vary their pitch, intonation, and emphasis to suit the words and dialects spoken by some of the animals so that drama and excitement are added to their oral interpretation. When everyone is comfortable with his or her passage, have the class make invitations to their reading. They might want to invite younger students, senior citizens, or their parents, for example. Ask the school's media specialist or a parent volunteer to videotape or tape-record the reading so students can see or listen to their performance later.

NAME ________________________________ DATE ____________

Which Way to Go?

Create a detailed map of Rabbit Hill, complete with each of the places mentioned in the novel. First establish north, south, east, and west, and draw a compass rose to indicate direction. Then establish your scale, such as 1 inch = 1 mile (1 cm = 1 km), and write it on the bottom of the map. Next, draw the map's outline. Include the garden, the farmhouse, and as many of the rabbits as you wish. On a separate paper, write directions telling how to get from one place to another using your map. Then trade your map and directions with a friend and see if you can each find your way.

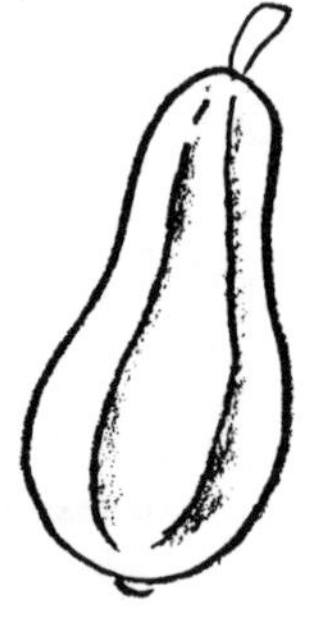

Roll of Thunder, Hear My Cry

MILDRED D. TAYLOR
(NEW YORK: DIAL PRESS, 1976)

ALL ABOUT THE BOOK

Roll of Thunder, Hear My Cry tells about a young black girl, Cassie Logan, who lives with her close-knit, loving family in rural Mississippi during the Depression. The Logans feel more secure than other black families because they own a farm. However, tension between the races builds when some white neighbors try to seize the Logans' land. Events climax when an angry mob of night riders tries to lynch T.J., a black teenager. Mr. Logan sets the cotton crop on fire to stop the lynching, and Cassie comes to understand the inequalities and hardships of her world. This book won the 1977 Newbery Medal.

CLASS ACTIVITY

Discuss with the class how Papa sacrifices the cotton crop and risks his life to save T.J. Then invite students to write an alternate ending to the novel. Explain to students that their new endings must also resolve all the threads of the plot and leave the reader feeling satisfied. Suggest that students begin by looking through the book and their notes to review the main events of the novel. When everyone has finished writing, have students share their new endings with the class.

NAME ______________________________ DATE ______________

Cassie's Future

What do you think will happen to Cassie when she grows up? How will her childhood shape her adult life? On the lines below, describe what Cassie's life might be like in ten years. You might want to tell about her education, job, home life, and friends, for example.

Sarah, Plain and Tall

PATRICIA MACLACHLAN
(NEW YORK: HARPER & ROW, 1985)

ALL ABOUT THE BOOK

Sarah, Plain and Tall, the 1986 Newbery Medal winner, tells of Anna and Caleb Witting and their life on the American prairie. Pa's wife dies giving birth to Caleb, and several years later he "advertises" for a new wife. Sarah Wheaton, a tall and plain woman from Maine, responds to the advertisement. The family tries hard to ease her adjustment to them and to the prairie. By the end of the book, Sarah becomes a permanent, beloved part of their lives as wife to Pa and mother to Anna and Caleb.

CLASS ACTIVITY

In *Sarah, Plain and Tall,* Papa places an advertisement in the newspaper for a wife. Explain to students that people place advertisements in newspapers, magazines, and journals for many different reasons. Explore with students how people use advertisements to buy items, sell items, announce services, ask for the return of lost pets, and so forth. Ask each student to cut out two newspaper advertisements and bring them to class. The next day, ask students to explain briefly to the class the purpose of the advertisements they clipped. Then have students write their own advertisement for something they wish to buy, sell, or announce.

NAME ______________________________ DATE ______________

Welcome to My Town!

Papa, Anna, and Caleb write letters to Sarah to tell her all about her new home. Then Sarah leaves her home in Maine to move to the prairie. Imagine that someone was moving to your town. What would you tell the person about your town? Create a brochure that would help people moving to your area feel welcome. To help you gather your ideas, first answer the questions listed below:

1. Where is your town located? ______________________________
2. How would you get there from a major city or airport? Give simple directions, using a map if you wish. ______________________________
3. What schools do you have in your area? ______________________________
4. What are the available activities and places for children? Include sports, music, parks, and clubs. ______________________________
5. What historic places are interesting to visit? ______________________________
6. What shopping areas are available? ______________________________
7. What are the best things about your town? ______________________________

Storms

SEYMOUR SIMON
(NEW YORK: MORROW, 1989)

ALL ABOUT THE BOOK

In *Storms,* Simon examines various kinds of devastating weather conditions, such as thunderstorms, hailstorms, tornadoes, and hurricanes, explaining how they form and why they die out. The author also tells readers how to protect themselves during these potentially deadly storms.

CLASS ACTIVITY

Suggest that students use *Storms* as a springboard for a study of meteorology. Have students form groups of two to three to research and report on different aspects of the topic. Possible areas for study include weather conditions, properties of the atmosphere, the history of meteorology, forecasting, climate, observation methods, and hurricanes and other weather phenomena. Students might also enjoy listening to weather forecasts on the news or gathering some from a newspaper and charting their accuracy over a week. After all the groups have completed their work, have students share their findings in panel discussions.

NAME ______________________ DATE ______________

Disaster!

Suppose you are a reporter sent to get the story on a hurricane that devastated a nearby area. You have inspected the damage, interviewed survivors, and spoken to rescue workers and other experts. In the space below, write your news story about the disaster. Remember that most news stories cover the 5 **W**'s and **H**: *who, what, when, where, why,* and *how.*

Tales Mummies Tell

PATRICIA LAUBER
(NEW YORK: CROWELL, 1985)

ALL ABOUT THE BOOK

Tales Mummies Tell is a fascinating study of mummies and what they reveal about people and creatures from the past. By X-raying and CAT-scanning mummies that have never been unwrapped, for example, scientists can discover a number of astonishing pieces of information, including a mummy's probable age at death, life style, diet, social class, diseases—even family relationships. Included are photographs of mummies of gerbils, bulls, crocodiles, and cats.

CLASS ACTIVITY

Have students work together to create a museum of their own, based on their reading of *Tales Mummies Tell.* Suggest they gather pictures of rare finds and valuable objects that have sparked controversy: King Tutankhamen's tomb, the Hope diamond, or the Rosetta stone, for example. Ask students to complete an index card for each picture, listing the object's name, place of origin, and importance. Then encourage students to arrange their "museum" and serve as "guides" as other classes visit. Encourage students to compile the index cards into a brochure for their museum.

NAME ____________________ DATE __________

A Mummy's Tale

Imagine *you* are one of the mummified people in *Tales Mummies Tell.* What was your life like? Use details from the book to help you describe how you lived. Include any details you need to complete your imaginative account. Write from the first person, using the pronoun *I*.

Volcano: The Eruption and Healing of Mount St. Helens

PATRICIA LAUBER
(NEW YORK: BRADBURY PRESS, 1986)

ALL ABOUT THE BOOK

Volcano: The Eruption and Healing of Mount St. Helens, a 1987 Newbery Honor Book, is a mesmerizing account of the 1980 eruption of Mount St. Helens in the state of Washington, which was all the more dramatic since the volcano had been quiescent for 123 years. The photographs that accompany the text are breathtaking.

CLASS ACTIVITY

The 1980 eruption of Mount St. Helens was so powerful that it blew off its entire summit, leaving a vast gaping caldera or crater. Geologists once thought that the primary cause of such volcanic activity was the introduction of water into the earth's highly heated core. Recently, however, scientists have come to believe that active volcanoes derive their energy from the movement of the earth's crustal plates.

Suggest that students form small groups to research and explain to the class how a volcano erupts, illustrating their presentation with charts and diagrams.

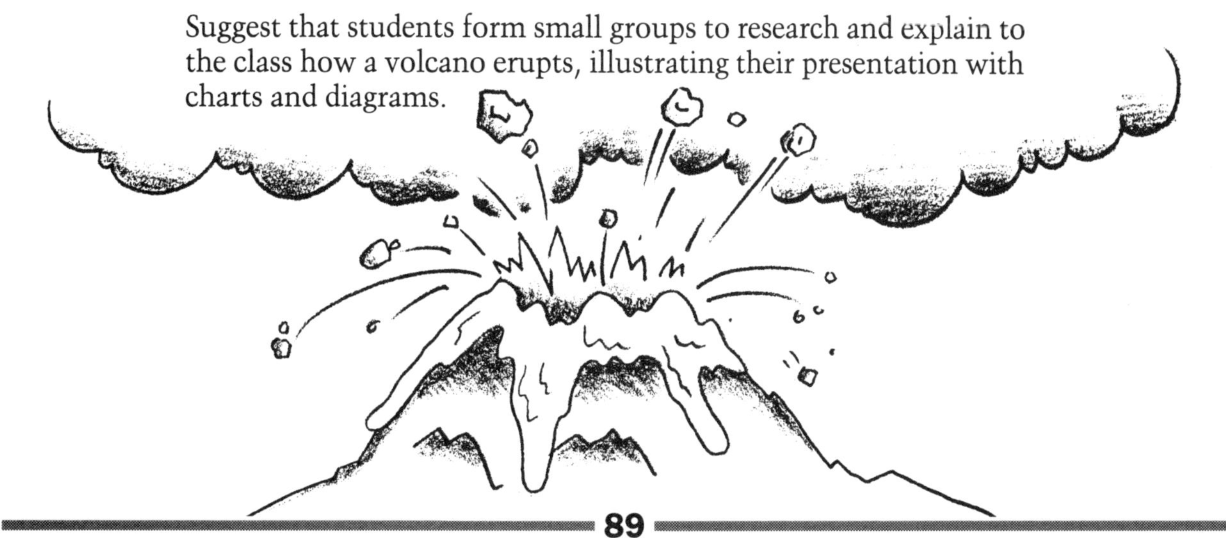

NAME ______________________________ DATE ______________

Volcano!

Select a well-known volcano, such as Etna (in Sicily), Stromboli (Italy), Vesuvius (Italy, near Naples), the Ring of Fire (volcanoes that encircle the Pacific Ocean), Krakatoa (Indonesia, between Java and Sumatra), or one of the Hawaiian volcanoes. Read about the volcano you chose. Then, in the space below, create a chart that describes the power of the eruption. Compare the speed of the lava flow, the volume of lava, and the force of the explosion with commonplace occurrences such as the speed of an automobile, the volume of a swimming pool, and the force of a bat hitting a ball. Consult an encyclopedia, almanac, or science book for help. Under your chart, write a brief description of what people should do to protect themselves from such an eruption.

Name of Volcano ____________	**Compared to . . .**
Speed of lava flow	
Volume of lava	
Force of explosion	

What People Should Do: ______________________________

____

When I Was Young in the Mountains

CYNTHIA RYLANT
ILLUSTRATED BY DIANE GOODE
(NEW YORK: DUTTON, 1982)

ALL ABOUT THE BOOK

When I Was Young in the Mountains recounts Rylant's childhood spent in her grandparents' Appalachian home. She reminisces fondly about enjoying a meal of steaming corn bread, pinto beans, and fried okra, going to the swimming hole, pumping well water into a tin bucket for her bath, shelling beans at night on the porch, and smelling the sweet milk at the general store. This book won a 1983 Caldecott Honor Award.

CLASS ACTIVITY

Remind students that *When I Was Young in the Mountains* is set in the Appalachian Mountains, an area noted for its rugged beauty. Point out to the class that today the Appalachians enjoy a brisk tourist business. Have students create a travel poster for the Appalachian Mountain area. Have a volunteer locate the area on a map of the United States. Use a travel guide, almanac, encyclopedia, and other reference material to explore with the class what this area might offer vacationers. Also suggest that students study the illustrations as well as the text to get ideas for their posters. Display the posters in the classroom and have students vote on the most effective one.

NAME ______________________________ DATE ______________

Dear Diary

Imagine you are the eight-year-old girl in Cynthia Rylant's *When I Was Young in the Mountains.* Think about how much she enjoys the simple pleasures of her life, such as her family's love and the wholesome food she eats. On the lines below, write a diary entry describing a typical day in the girl's life in the mountains. Remember to use the pronoun *I.*

Wilma Rudolph: Champion Athlete

TOM BIRACREE
(NEW YORK: CHELSEA HOUSE, 1989)

ALL ABOUT THE BOOK

Wilma Rudolph: Champion Athlete traces the life of the track star. Although stricken with polio at the age of four and unable to walk without a metal leg brace until she was about twelve, Rudolph went on to become the first American woman to win three gold medals in the Olympic running events. Called "the fastest woman alive," Rudolph's dignified struggle against poverty, racism, and illness has provided inspiration for countless young athletes of all backgrounds.

CLASS ACTIVITY

Suggest that students research poliomyelitis, the disease that Rudolph so courageously overcame. Begin by reminding them how widespread the disease once was. In the early 1950s, about a decade after Rudolph contracted the disease, nearly 60,000 people contracted polio; most victims were children between the ages of five and ten. Suggest that students work in small groups to research such subtopics as symptoms, treatment, disease control, and vaccination. Have students write brief reports to share their findings with the class.

NAME ______________________ DATE ____________

Dear Folks . . .

As Wilma Rudolph learned, fame has both good and bad sides. Imagine that you are Wilma after your 1960 Olympic victory. Write a letter home to your parents, explaining how you feel about your victory, your teammates, and your friends. Include both the positive and negative experiences of your victory.

______________________,

____

____

____

____

____

____

____

____

____

____

____

____

____

____

______________________,

The Witch of Blackbird Pond

ELIZABETH GEORGE SPEARE
(BOSTON: HOUGHTON MIFFLIN, 1958)

ALL ABOUT THE BOOK

The Witch of Blackbird Pond is set in colonial Connecticut in 1687. Sixteen-year-old Katherine (''Kit'') Tyler travels from Barbados to Wethersfield, Connecticut, where her unconventional upbringing and luxurious wardrobe are out of place in her aunt's Puritan household. In the meadows by Blackbird Pond she meets and befriends the lonely Hannah Tupper, a widow regarded by the colonists as a witch. A local family, the Cruffs, charge Kit with witchcraft when they find out that she has been secretly teaching their daughter Prudence to read. Kit is exonerated of all charges when Goodman Cruff stands up to his wife and withdraws his accusation. This book won the Newbery Medal in 1959.

CLASS ACTIVITY

Aside from the witchcraft hysteria, colonial America was rife with disease, animal attacks, and food shortages. Nonetheless, people flocked to American shores. In part, they were persuaded to make the perilous journey and to undergo the challenges of resettlement through various advertisements. Have students write their own advertisements to entice people of the Old World to come to colonial America. First ask students to brainstorm a list of lures that would attract people to America. Guide them to see the appeal of adventure, vast tracts of land, abundant game for food and furs, and religious freedom. Suggest they create their advertisements in poster format. Display the posters for others to share.

NAME ______________________ DATE ______________

News Flash!

Imagine that you are a newscaster sent to interview people as their ships land in colonial America. Whom would you pick to interview? What questions would you ask? In the spaces below, write your questions and the person's answers.

The name of the person you are interviewing: ______________________

Age: ______________ Occupation: ______________________

Appearance: ______________________

Question: ______________________

Answer: ______________________

Question: ______________________

Answer: ______________________

Question: ______________________

Answer: ______________________

Question: ______________________

Answer: ______________________